WHALES

Created and Written by
John Bonnett Wexo

Zoological Consultant
Charles R. Schroeder, D.V.M.
Director Emeritus
San Diego Zoo &
San Diego Wild Animal Park

Scientific Consultants
Vladimir S. Gurevich, Ph.D.
Marine Biologist, Consultant

Sylvia Earle, Ph.D.
Research Biologist
California Academy of Sciences

Albert C. Myrick, Ph.D.
Wildlife Biologist
National Marine Fisheries Service

Ronn Storro-Patterson, M.A.
Research Director
The Whale Center, San Francisco

Creative Education

Published by Creative Education, Inc., 123 South Broad Street, Mankato, Minnesota 56001

Printed by permission of Wildlife Education, Ltd.

ISBN 0-88682-272-6

Contents

Whales live in the ocean like fish. They swim around and hunt in the ocean like fish. They even look something like fish. But they are *not* fish. They are mammals, like you and me.

A mammal is an animal that has lungs and breathes air. It is warm-blooded, with a body temperature that is more or less the same all the time. The babies of mammals are born alive instead of hatched from eggs. And the babies take milk from their mothers. Whales are mammals that live in the sea — sea mammals.

Scientists call all whales cetaceans (SEE-TAY-SHUNS), which means "whales." But there are really *two* rather different groups of whales. The Killer whale on page 16 belongs to a group that scientists call the Odontoceti (o-DON-TUH-SEE-TEE), which means "toothed whales."

The Humpback whale shown below belongs to a group that is commonly called the baleen (BAY-LEEN) whales. Scientists call this group the Mysticeti (MISS-TUH-SEE-TEE), which means "whales with mustaches." Both names refer to the baleen of these whales, a strange feeding apparatus that looks like a mustache — but this mustache is *inside* the mouth!

In both groups of whales, males are called bulls. Females are called cows. And a young whale is called a calf.

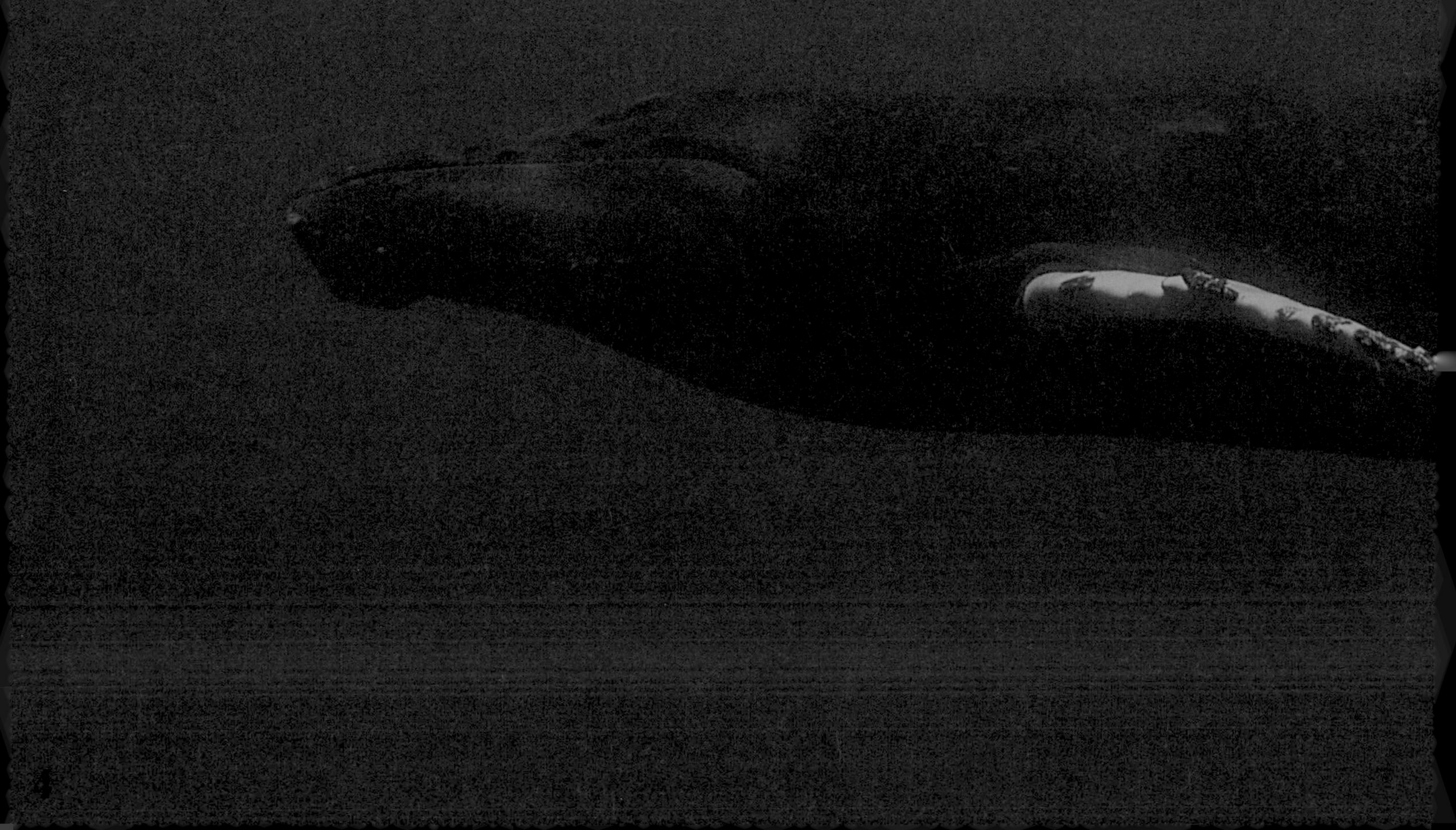

5

Baleen whales can be very big. The largest of them, the Blue whale, can be over 100 feet long (30.5 meters). But there are whales in this group that are much smaller. Some baleen whales never grow any longer than 20 feet (6 meters).

It is not *size* that determines which whales are included in this group. It is *the way that they catch their food.* All baleen whales filter (or strain) small animals out of ocean water. Sometimes, they catch small fish in this way. But mostly, they catch very small animals called plankton. In certain parts of the ocean, billions of tiny plankton float near the water's surface, and baleen whales go there to feed.

Blue whales are the biggest animals that have ever lived on earth. They are over 6 times bigger than the biggest brontosaurus that ever lived. And they make elephants look really small. A Blue whale can weigh as much as *32 elephants!*

The two "wings" on the end of a whale's tail are called flukes (FLEWks). When a whale is swimming, the flukes push against the water a lot, so they must be very tough. Strong fibers are densely packed inside the flukes to make them almost as strong as steel. In fact, you could hang a huge whale up by its flukes and they would not break.

All of the power for pushing a whale forward comes from its tail. For this reason, the muscles in the tail are the largest in a whale's body. Think of the power it takes to push a whale weighing 300 thousand pounds (136,000 kilograms) through the water!

Blowhole

Lungs

Whales are mammals, so they must breathe air. They can dive under the water, but they must always return to the surface for air. A whale's nose is called a "blowhole." It is on top of the whale's head, so the whale can breathe without coming very far out of the water.

Cold Water

Blubber

Warm

Whales often swim in very cold water. To help them stay warm, they have a thick layer of fat around their bodies. This is called "blubber." It acts like an overcoat to keep heat inside the body from escaping.

A human skeleton usually weighs less than 25 pounds (11 kilograms). The skeleton of a Blue whale can weigh more than *50 thousand pounds* (22,680 kilograms).

Some baleen whales feed by sifting plankton directly out of the water. They swim along close to the surface with their mouths open. Plankton float into the mouth and are caught on the baleen. These whales are called "skimmers."

① The baleen in a whale's mouth hangs down like the teeth of a comb. The pieces of baleen overlap a little, and have fringe along one side. When a gulper feeds, water and plankton are sucked into the mouth 1. Then the throat contracts, pushing the tongue up. This forces the water out through the baleen 2. The plankton are caught on the fringed edges of the baleen and swallowed.

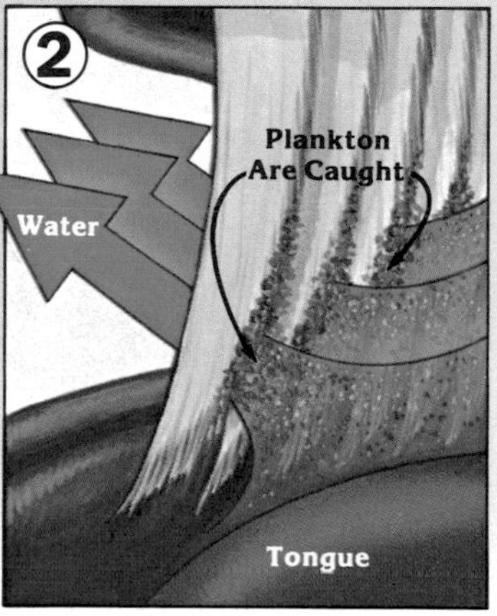

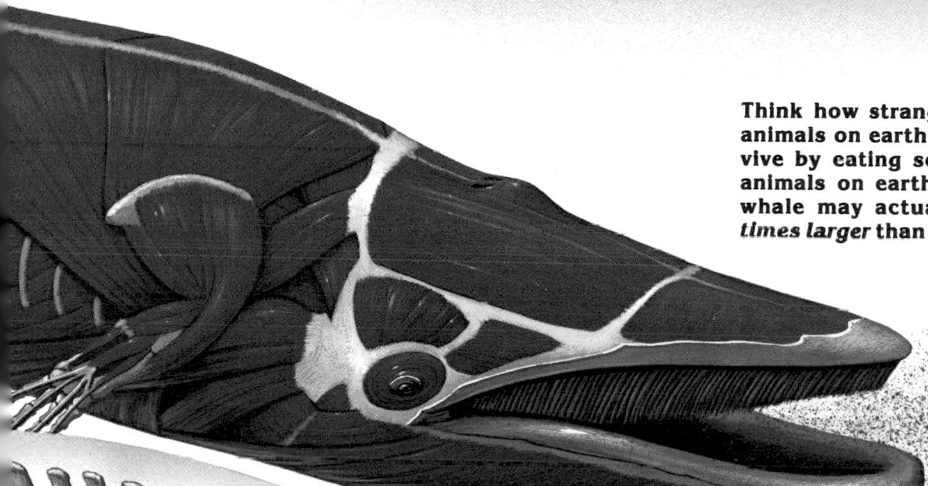

Baleen

Plankton and Water

② Water

Plankton Are Caught

Tongue

Other baleen whales are called "gulpers." This is because they start feeding by gulping huge amounts of water and plankton into their mouths. Their pleated throats bulge out to hold it all. (To see what happens next, look at the diagrams at right.)

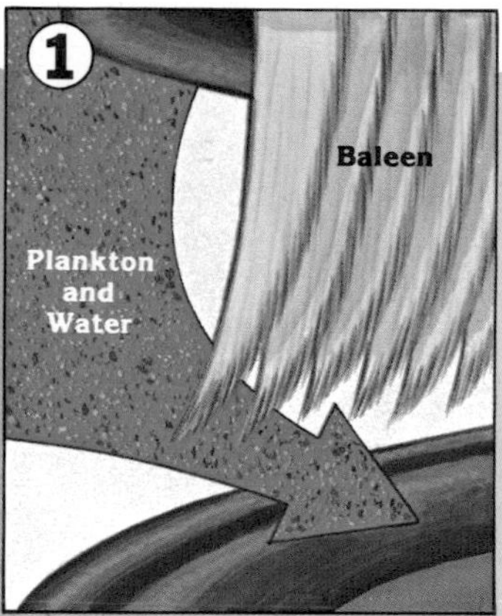

Think how strange it is. The largest animals on earth (baleen whales) survive by eating some of the smallest animals on earth (plankton). A Blue whale may actually be *100 million times larger* than the food it eats.

The largest of the plankton are called krill (shown above). They may grow to be 2 inches long (6 centimeters). Most plankton are much smaller. Some are so small that you would need a magnifying glass to see them.

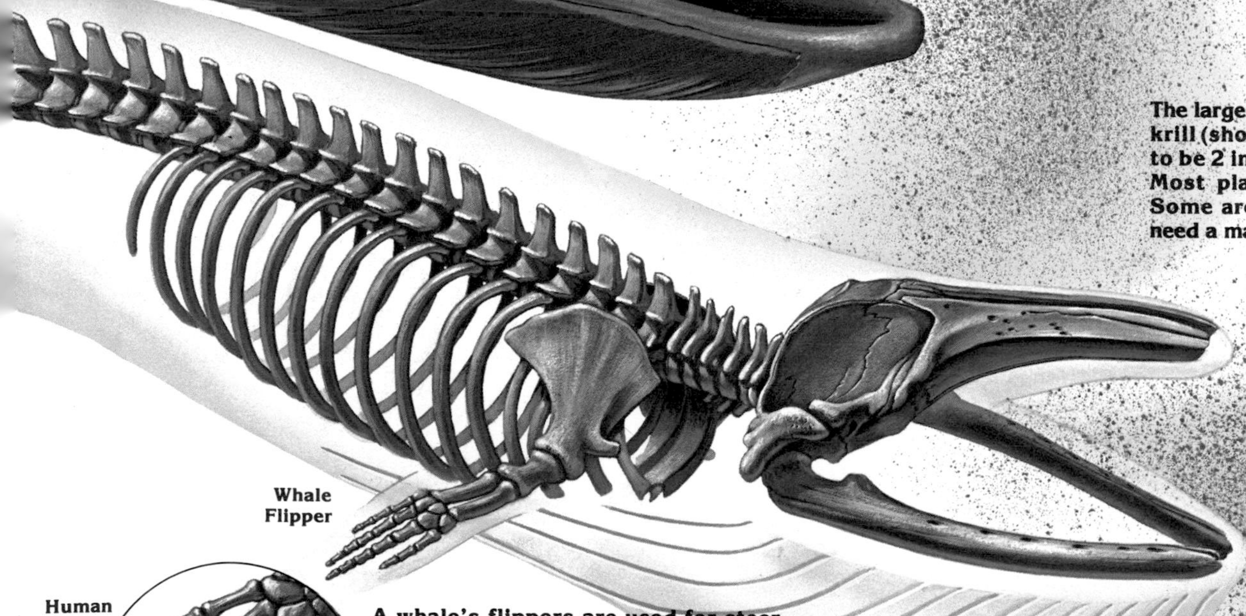

Whale Flipper

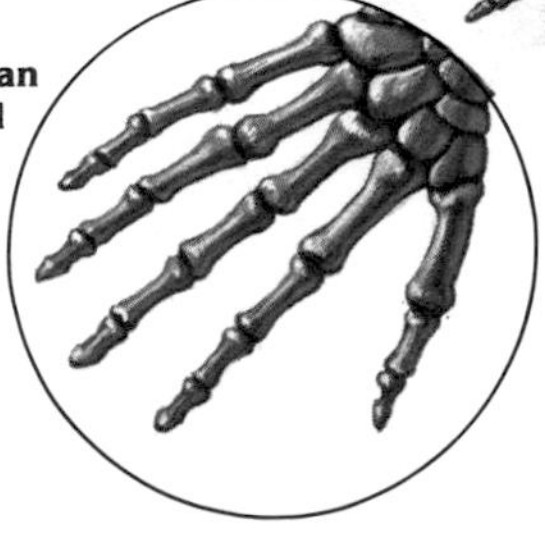

Human Hand

A whale's flippers are used for steering. On the outside, they are smooth and rounded like paddles. But the bones inside the flippers look very much like the bones inside your fingers. Blue whales have only four of these "fingers," but most whales have five.

A large Blue whale can eat more than 9,000 pounds of food a day (4,100 kilograms). Every time it swallows, over 100 pounds of food can go down its throat (50 kilograms).

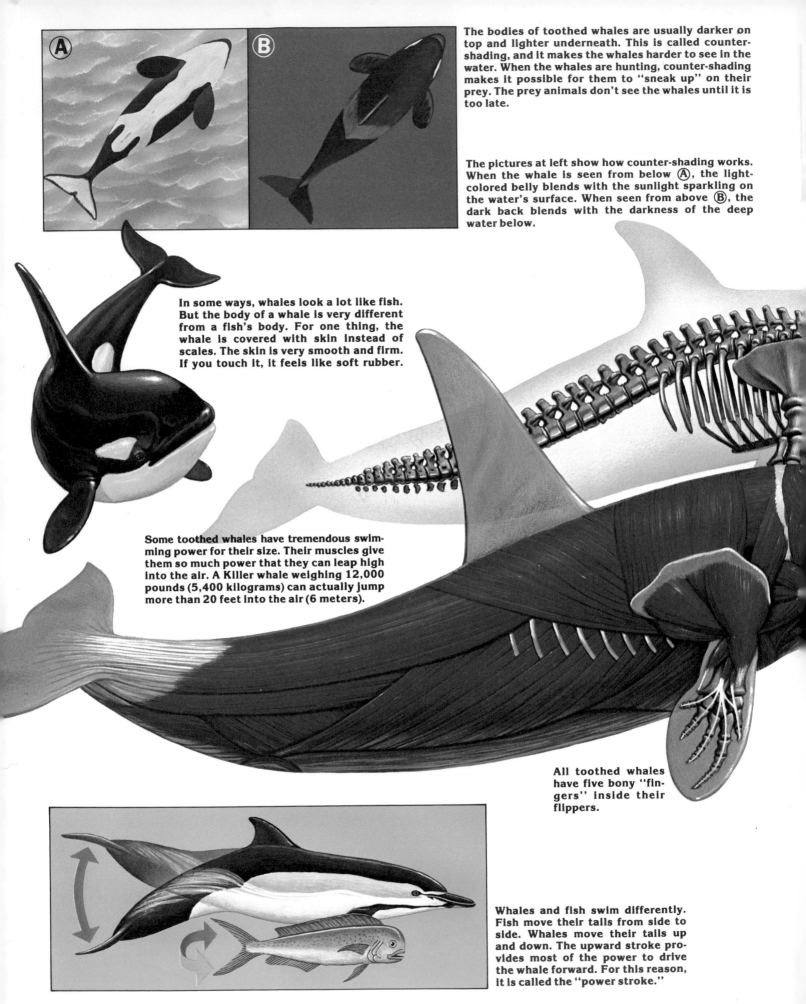

The bodies of toothed whales are usually darker on top and lighter underneath. This is called counter-shading, and it makes the whales harder to see in the water. When the whales are hunting, counter-shading makes it possible for them to "sneak up" on their prey. The prey animals don't see the whales until it is too late.

The pictures at left show how counter-shading works. When the whale is seen from below Ⓐ, the light-colored belly blends with the sunlight sparkling on the water's surface. When seen from above Ⓑ, the dark back blends with the darkness of the deep water below.

In some ways, whales look a lot like fish. But the body of a whale is very different from a fish's body. For one thing, the whale is covered with skin instead of scales. The skin is very smooth and firm. If you touch it, it feels like soft rubber.

Some toothed whales have tremendous swimming power for their size. Their muscles give them so much power that they can leap high into the air. A Killer whale weighing 12,000 pounds (5,400 kilograms) can actually jump more than 20 feet into the air (6 meters).

All toothed whales have five bony "fingers" inside their flippers.

Whales and fish swim differently. Fish move their tails from side to side. Whales move their tails up and down. The upward stroke provides most of the power to drive the whale forward. For this reason, it is called the "power stroke."

  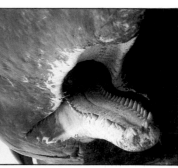

Different types of toothed whales have different types of teeth. In general, the size and shape of a whale's teeth are related to the size and type of prey that the whale must catch. Killer whales, for example, sometimes take large sea mammals like seals and walruses. Their teeth are thick and heavy.

The *number* of teeth in a whale's mouth is also related to the type of prey that the whale catches. The Bottlenose dolphin (above, left) feeds mainly on small and slippery fish. To help it grab and hold such prey, it has lots of sharp little teeth—as many as 100 of them. The False Killer whale (above, right) catches larger fish and squid. It has larger teeth and fewer of them.

Sperm whales are the biggest toothed whales, and they catch the biggest prey. They have the biggest teeth. All of the teeth are in the lower jaw. When the whale closes its mouth, the teeth fit into sockets in the upper jaw.

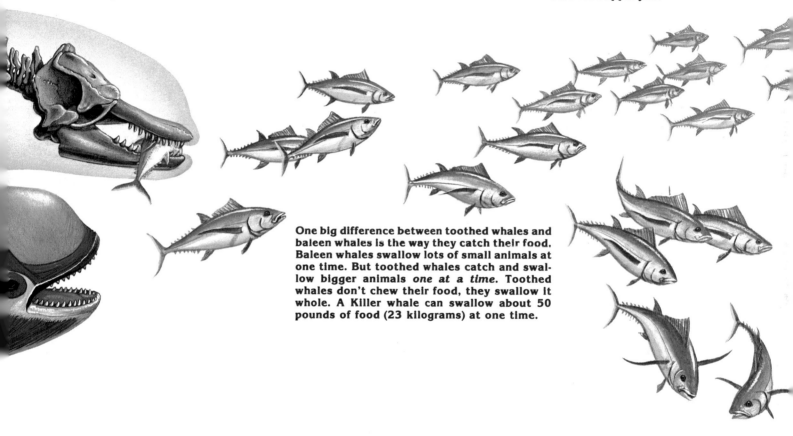

One big difference between toothed whales and baleen whales is the way they catch their food. Baleen whales swallow lots of small animals at one time. But toothed whales catch and swallow bigger animals *one at a time*. Toothed whales don't chew their food, they swallow it whole. A Killer whale can swallow about 50 pounds of food (23 kilograms) at one time.

Toothed whales are much smaller as a rule than baleen whales. It is true that the largest of the toothed whales, the Sperm whale, may be 69 feet long (21 meters). And the second largest toothed whale, the Killer whale, may be more than 32 feet long (9.75 meters). But most toothed whales are between 10 and 20 feet long (3 and 6 meters). And the smallest of the group is only 3 feet long (1 meter).

The difference in size between toothed whales and baleen whales may have to do with the ways that the two groups get their food. Baleen whales don't have to do much active swimming to feed themselves. They just cruise along gathering up plankton. Toothed whales must actively chase their prey, and large size could slow them down.

As a rule, toothed whales are excellent hunters. They often work together in groups to round up prey, in the same way that lions or wolves cooperate when they hunt. Groups of Killer whales have been known to capture large Polar bears, and to attack huge Blue whales.

Toothed whales are the whales that most people know best, because they are the whales that are seen in shows. The size and learning abilities of these whales make them ideal for shows. You may know them as dolphins or porpoises (PORE-PUS-IZ) — but they are all toothed whales.

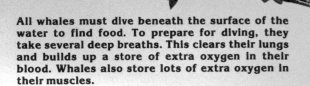

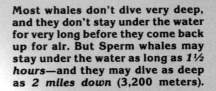

All whales must dive beneath the surface of the water to find food. To prepare for diving, they take several deep breaths. This clears their lungs and builds up a store of extra oxygen in their blood. Whales also store lots of extra oxygen in their muscles.

Most whales don't dive very deep, and they don't stay under the water for very long before they come back up for air. But Sperm whales may stay under the water as long as *1½ hours*—and they may dive as deep as *2 miles down* (3,200 meters).

The Bottlenose dolphin (shown below) is the toothed whale that is most often seen in shows. When you see it streaking around a pool and leaping through the air, it seems incredibly fast and graceful. But the Bottlenose is not even close to being the fastest of the whales. The top speed for a Bottlenose is around 18 miles per hour (29 kilometers per hour). The Common dolphin has been seen swimming as fast as 70 miles per hour (113 kilometers per hour).

Far below the surface of the sea, Sperm whales find one of their favorite foods—giant squid. These huge sea monsters are as long as the whales that hunt them, and terrific fights between whales and squid must take place in the dark depths of the ocean.

FOLD OUT ▶

Whales can "see" with their ears.

If you have ever tried to open your eyes in the ocean, you know why whales really can't depend on their eyes to find their way around. It's hard to see anything under water. Even in "clear" water, you can't see much farther than 200 feet (60 meters). And the deeper you go under the surface, the less light there is. At a depth of 1,300 feet (400 meters), the ocean is pitch black.

Luckily for whales, water carries *sound* much better than it carries *light*. Sound travels more than four times faster in water than it does in air —and it travels much farther, too. Some whales have been able to take advantage of this to "see" with sound. The process is called echo-location, and some whales that use it can "see" much farther under water than you can see in air! For a simple explanation of how it works, look below.

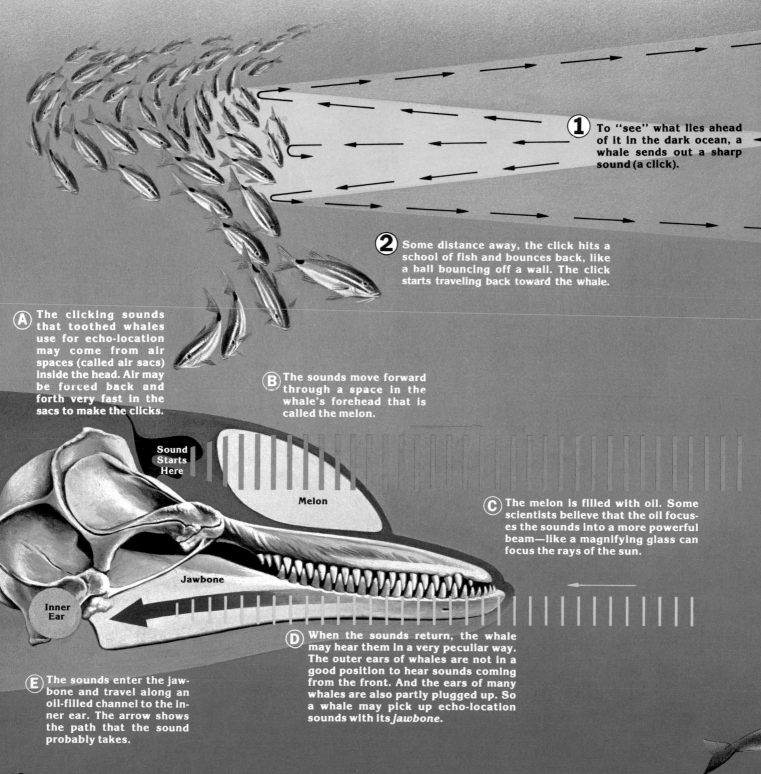

1 To "see" what lies ahead of it in the dark ocean, a whale sends out a sharp sound (a click).

2 Some distance away, the click hits a school of fish and bounces back, like a ball bouncing off a wall. The click starts traveling back toward the whale.

A The clicking sounds that toothed whales use for echo-location may come from air spaces (called air sacs) inside the head. Air may be forced back and forth very fast in the sacs to make the clicks.

B The sounds move forward through a space in the whale's forehead that is called the melon.

C The melon is filled with oil. Some scientists believe that the oil focuses the sounds into a more powerful beam—like a magnifying glass can focus the rays of the sun.

D When the sounds return, the whale may hear them in a very peculiar way. The outer ears of whales are not in a good position to hear sounds coming from the front. And the ears of many whales are also partly plugged up. So a whale may pick up echo-location sounds with its *jawbone*.

E The sounds enter the jawbone and travel along an oil-filled channel to the inner ear. The arrow shows the path that the sound probably takes.

Sound Starts Here

Melon

Jawbone

Inner Ear

ELKHART LAKE I M C

Sound travels very fast in water. It can travel almost a mile (1,500 meters) in one second. For this reason, a whale can "see" a school of fish almost a mile away in only two seconds. (It takes one second for the sound to travel to the fish, and one second for it to travel back to the whale.)

Scientific tests have shown that toothed whales can do some wonderful things with echo-location. Dolphins can tell one shape from another, even in muddy water or in complete darkness. They can tell a circle from a triangle, for example—or a smaller circle from a larger circle.

3 The sound comes back to the whale. If it takes a long time for the click to go out and come back, the whale knows the fish are far away. If it takes a short time, the whale knows that the fish are close.

Even more remarkable, dolphins can tell what something is *made* of without touching it and without using their eyes. From a hundred feet away, blindfolded dolphins can tell if a square is made of metal, wood, or plastic!

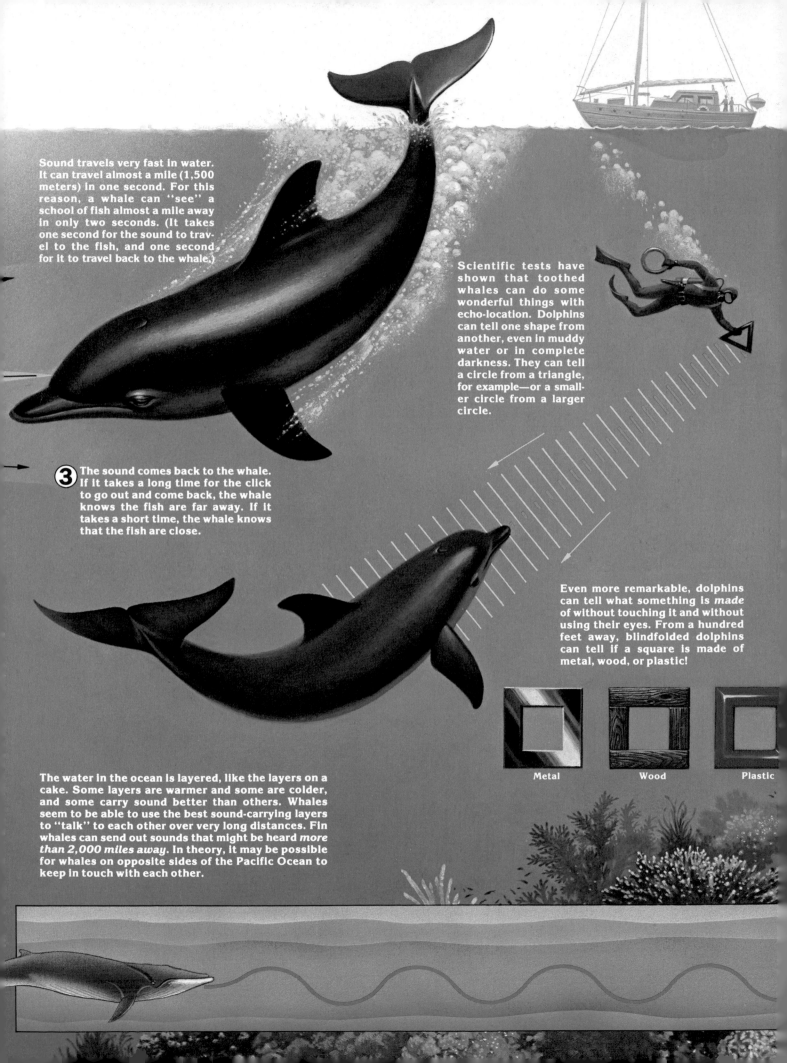

Metal   Wood   Plastic

The water in the ocean is layered, like the layers on a cake. Some layers are warmer and some are colder, and some carry sound better than others. Whales seem to be able to use the best sound-carrying layers to "talk" to each other over very long distances. Fin whales can send out sounds that might be heard *more than 2,000 miles away.* In theory, it may be possible for whales on opposite sides of the Pacific Ocean to keep in touch with each other.

Sometimes, whales are stranded on a beach and die. For no apparent reason, a group of whales may swim into very shallow water near a beach. When the tide goes out, they are left high and dry. Nobody is sure why these mass strandings occur, but some scientists feel that the echo-location systems of the whales may not be working correctly. As a result of this, the whales may become confused about where they are, and swim into shallow waters that they would usually avoid.

In addition to finding food, whales probably use echo-location for finding their way around in the ocean. When a whale is close to land, the ability to see what's ahead is particularly important. By sending out clicks, a whale can probably tell when it is too close to rocks or other dangerous places.

Are whales really intelligent?

There are some scientists who feel that some types of whales may be as intelligent as people are. There are a few scientists who believe that whales may be *more* intelligent than people. And there are some who feel that whales are no more intelligent than dogs.

A lot of facts have been collected about whale intelligence—but it's hard to decide what the facts really *mean*. For example, it's a fact that some whales have very large brains. The Sperm whale has the largest brain of any animal that has ever lived. It can weigh as much as 20 pounds (9 kilograms), which is *four times* bigger than the biggest human brain.

But does *size* tell you anything about how *good* a brain is? Among humans, Albert Einstein probably had the best brain of all. But Einstein's brain was not the biggest human brain of all.

What about the *structure* of whale brains —the way the brains are made? Can this tell us anything about how good the brains are? Scientists have studied human brains and found that certain parts of the brain are related to certain kinds of activity. The front part of the brain, for example, has to do with thinking.

The front part of many whale brains is very large. Some dolphins have many more brain cells in this area than humans do. But we really don't know whether whales *use* these cells in the same way that humans do. We don't know whether they use them for thinking, or for something we can't even imagine.

And this is the main problem that we must face in trying to say how intelligent whales may be. Their lives are so different from ours that intelligence in their lives may be very different from what we call intelligence in our lives.

We live on land, whales live in water. We have hands and work with tools, while they have no hands and no tools. We build buildings and machines, while they survive very well without them.

If we ever do learn to "talk" with whales, we may learn that whales are not "more intelligent" than us or "less intelligent," but simply *different from us*.

Dolphin Brain

Human Brain

Some scientists believe that the amount of folding on the front part of the brain shows the amount of intelligence that a creature has. Dolphins have twice as many folds as people do.

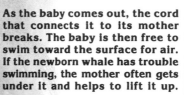

Baby whales are born differently from almost all other mammals. They are born under water. For this reason, a baby whale doesn't breathe while it is being born. If it did, water would get into its lungs and it would drown.

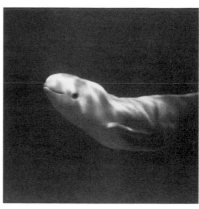

As the baby comes out, the cord that connects it to its mother breaks. The baby is then free to swim toward the surface for air. If the newborn whale has trouble swimming, the mother often gets under it and helps to lift it up.

As soon as it reaches the surface, the baby starts to breathe. Later, it starts to take milk from its mother, like all mammals do. The milk is very rich and baby whales grow very fast. With the larger whales, the growth can be truly amazing. During the first 7 months after it is born, a Blue whale can gain about *33 thousand pounds* (15,000 kilograms). It can put on weight at the rate of 10 pounds an hour!

Many people have seen whales trying to help other whales. As shown above, a group of dolphins will sometimes work together to keep the blowhole of a sick dolphin above water, so it can continue to breathe. If the dolphin's blowhole were allowed to slip under the water, it would drown. Some scientists say this is intelligent social behavior. Others say it is simply instinct.

Some whales seem to do very "intelligent" things when they feed. Humpback whales, for example, sometimes catch krill or fish in a "bubble net." To do this, one or two whales swim in a circle around a school of fish. As they swim, they blow bubbles. The bubbles frighten the fish, and they flee to the center of the circle. Then the Humpbacks simply swim up the middle of the bubble net and swallow most of the fish.

The ability to learn by imitating others is often considered to be a sign of intelligence. Dolphins, Killer whales, and other toothed whales are famous for their ability to learn and perform tricks. And they don't stop there. Often, when they are bored they will make up new tricks of their own.

The future of whales depends on what people do. Many types of whales are extremely close to extinction, including the Blue whale and other large whales. And people are responsible for this. For hundreds of years, people have hunted and killed whales for their meat and oil. Today, this is no longer necessary. We have better sources for oil and meat—sources that do not require the killing of magnificent whales. And yet, there are still some people who want to go on killing whales, because they can make money doing it.

Fortunately, there are many other people who want to *stop* the killing of whales. These people have joined together in groups that are working to help save whales. If you would like to help whales, we hope that you will write to some of the groups listed below. They will tell you how you can help.

**American Association
of Zoological Parks & Aquariums**
Oglebay Park
Wheeling, West Virginia 26003

American Cetacean Society
P. O. Box 4416
San Pedro, California 90731

Elsa Wild Animal Appeal
P. O. Box 4572
North Hollywood, California 91607

Friends of the Earth
1045 Sansome Street
San Francisco, California 94111

Hubbs Sea World Research Institute
1700 South Shores Rd.
San Diego, California 92109

National Wildlife Federation
1412 Sixteenth Street, N. W.
Washington, D. C. 20036

Project Jonah
P. O. Box 40280
San Francisco, California 94140

The Whale Center
3929 Piedmont Avenue
Oakland, California 94611

The Whale Protection Fund
624 Ninth Street
Washington, D. C. 20001

World Wildlife Fund
1601 Connecticut Avenue, N. W.
Washington, D. C. 20009

Index

Index

Art Credits

Pages Four and Five: Mark Hallett; **Pages Six and Seven:** Barbara Hoopes; **Page Six: Upper Right,** Walter Stuart; **Lower Left,** Walter Stuart; **Page Seven: Upper Right,** Walter Stuart, **Pages Eight and Nine:** Barbara Hoopes; **Page Eight: Upper Left,** Walter Stuart; **Lower Left,** Ron Stark; **Page Nine:** Ron Stark; **Pages Ten and Eleven:** Mark Hallett and Barbara Hoopes; **Pages Twelve and Thirteen:** Davis Meltzer; **Pages Twelve and Thirteen: Bottom,** Walter Stuart; **Pages Fourteen and Fifteen:** Walter Stuart; **Page Fifteen: Lower Right,** James Teason; **Pages Sixteen and Seventeen:** Walter Stuart.

Photographic Credits

Front Cover: Francois Gohier *(Ardea London);* **Pages Four and Five:** Ed Robinson *(Tom Stack and Associates);* **Page Seven:** Inigo Everson *(Bruce Coleman, Ltd.);* **Page Nine: Left,** Francois Gohier *(Ardea London);* **Middle,** Jonathan T. Wright *(Bruce Coleman, Inc.);* **Right,** Ken Balcomb *(Bruce Coleman, Ltd.);* **Page Nine:** Maurice Landre *(Freelance Photographers Guild);* **Page Thirteen:** T. A. Gornall, D.V.M.; **Page Fifteen: Top,** Jeremy Fitzgibbon *(Vancouver Public Aquarium);* **Far Right,** Hans de Jager *(Vancouver Public Aquarium);* **Center,** Peter Hulbert *(Vancouver Public Aquarium);* **Lower Left,** Jen and Des Bartlett *(Bruce Coleman, Inc.);* **Pages Sixteen and Seventeen:** Wardene Weisser *(Bruce Coleman, Inc.).*

Our Thanks To: Steve and May Lou Swartz *(Cetacean Research Associates);* Rick Geissler; Stan Minasian *(Marine Mammal Fund);* Pete Laurie; Don Wilke *(Scripps Aquarium-Museum);* Stefanie Hewlett *(Vancouver Public Aquarium);* Ray Gilmore and Don Hughes *(San Diego Natural History Museum);* Diana McIntyre *(Los Angeles County Museum of Natural History);* William Perrin *(National Marine Fisheries);* Lynnette Wexo.

This book is dedicated to Noah Wexo, whose love and patience helped to make it possible.

Creative Education would like to thank Wildlife Education, Ltd., for granting them the rights to print and distribute this hardbound edition.